DON'T RETIRE
REJUVENATE

MICHAEL MIDDLETON

CONTENTS

ABOUT THE AUTHOR

Michael Middleton is a financial planner with over thirty years of experience advising private individuals, entrepreneurs and company executives on a range of issues. This is his second book on the issue of retirement planning, or more specifically on the non financial aspects of retirement.

As the title suggests the author sees a future in which retirement as we have viewed it conventionally either has or will begin to disappear. His first book on the subject, The R Word Time to Retire Retirement has given rise to a workshop together with a series of tools to help people consider or as he puts it "re imagineer" their future.

ACKNOWLEDGEMENTS

As always even a short book such as this cannot be completed without help, so my thanks for their patience and attention must go, in no particular order to, Cornerstone Literary Agency and Nick Hermann for their work on the manuscript, Louise Chamberlain at H2 Creative for putting the final piece together and getting it set up properly for printing and publication.

Of course, those many people I have queried, quizzed and bored on the subject of not retiring must also be acknowledged as without feedback on my ideas nothing could have been done. Too many to note individually, but they know who they are.

CHAPTER ONE

INTRODUCTION

One of the key problems with the concept of retirement, or rather how we see it, is the sense that somehow our lives as we knew them have come to an end. Although there may be multiple causes that contribute to our view of retirement, we can simplify the issue to one focal point: our mindset. Our mindsets on the subject of retirement get an early start, as we perhaps spend time with grandparents as babies, who unlike mum and dad seem to have plenty of time on their hands – often with little to do and all day to do it in.

For the purposes of this short book, I define retirement as a time when we cease to work and withdraw from an active life – this can frequently be due to having reached a particular age. Again, for the purposes of the book, I assume that the normal age at which this event takes place is between the ages of 60 and 65. Some people refer to retirement as one of life's "stages".

There are many claims as to the origin of the term "life stages" from people in business and marketing, using the term to promote their services to various state institutions across education, healthcare and social services, seeking to find neat boxes into which life can be fitted.

There may be some logic to this, but as we learn more and more about less and less, many of these definitions begin to appear oversimplified. For example, a UK-based course in social care notes "The Six Life Stages": infancy, early childhood, adolescence, early adulthood, middle adulthood and later adulthood. Within the course outlines, there are some broad descriptions as to what happens to us in terms of health and physiology in each stage. It notes that the ageing process begins during middle adulthood. My first challenge to this convention I will note is this – namely that we age from the moment we are born.

To understand how to make the most of our lives, and realise the abundance of opportunity we have, it is first necessary to ditch institutional language and concepts. Simply put, the modern world is changing too fast for us to be neatly placed into stages. If we allow this to happen to us, at least in terms of the way we think, we are in effect being put into a box. If our thinking is organised along these lines, then in order to progress our lives we first need to climb out of one box in order to get into the next. Life becomes one long struggle to get in and out of boxes. Not only is this a wholly negative view of the way we live today, it ignores the very simple fact that life is a continuum – a long series of transitions from birth to death.

One academic article on this area, written by Jeffery Jensen Arnett of Clark University in Worcester Massachusetts, identifies how when early psychologists such as Sigmund Freud first proposed theories of life stages, it caused debate and a great many challenges, which largely continue today. In his paper 'Human Development', Dr. Arnett also notes how much older civilisations used the idea of life stages, which when contrasted with some modern claims, shows how humans have long sought to organise our thinking around age – what we can do at certain ages and what our roles and responsibilities are at each stage.

This might have served a certain purpose in the organisation of cultures and societies of the past, but how relevant is this thinking today? I would say, categorically, it is not. If we bring a form of terminology into our everyday life, such as the notion of retirement, soon its everyday use, when repeated often enough, becomes part of our mindset. That fixed mindset forces us to feel considerable discomfort when we arrive at retirement – we expect our lives to move from one stage to another only to discover we either cannot, or the goal posts have moved. In turn this can create extremely negative views of our world and our place within it.

Life stages are of great help to those studying, researching and developing new medicines and technologies, but they are of no help to anyone seeking to make the maximum productive use of their lives.

In the introduction to an article aimed at businesses entitled 'The Bionic Company', The Boston Consulting Group makes the following observation:

New technologies operate at superhuman speed. Social, political, and economic forces move much more slowly. To use learning as a competitive advantage, companies must be able to learn on both timescales.

Whilst this may not seem relevant to issues surrounding retirement, the piece serves to reinforce the challenge we face when it comes to changing our thinking. For the Baby Boomers retiring today, the world they face is changing rapidly, yet there is a tendency or even a desire to hold on to the things they find comfortable and grew up with. However, a fulfilling and purposeful retirement cannot be achieved using the mindsets of the past. It is essential to think differently and to live differently – in doing so, life beyond normal retirement age holds many wonderful opportunities.

Throughout this book, I will make reference to the Japanese concept of *Ikigai*. The Japanese do not have a direct translation for the word "retirement", however they do have the term *Ikigai*, which roughly translates to "your reason for getting up in the morning." *Ikigai* is widely practised throughout Japan. It is a powerful and useful concept, not only in terms of living in later life, but in organising how we transition through life. However, there are aspects of the lives of those people who follow the practice of *Ikigai*, especially in Okinawa, that make it impossible to absolutely replicate elsewhere in the world. Primarily this comes down to the combination of climate and diet. The Okinawans' have access to particular vegetables that are not found elsewhere. The best we can do is to learn from the attitudes and mindsets that *Ikigai* promotes, and adapt the concept to fit our own circumstances. Okinawa is home to the largest number of centenarians per capita in the world.

Something is clearly working well.

In the western world, the idea of life stages is fixed in us from a very early age and dominates the way we educate our children. I was born in 1961, and my early education taught me that I was to experience a number of stages: firstly the need to develop basic skills, followed by schooling, further education, a career and then retirement. Each step was a preparation for the next, with retirement being sold as a welcome respite from a lifetime of back-breaking work. My family roots are in the north of England – they were not prosperous. Prosperity was something that happened to others – a lucky few – so I came to understand that retirement was synonymous with being old and exhausted.

By the time I reached my late teens, a more appealing notion of retirement had begun to emerge: one that was more Hollywood than the coal slag heaps that surrounded my grandparent's home in the North. Despite this new-found optimism that ordinary people could enjoy a prosperous life, the idea reinforced by Hollywood and glossy magazines was still problematic – in order to enjoy the glamour it would be necessary to "retire" earlier, probably by my fifties, in order to have enough time to enjoy the accumulated wealth. It was with this image, and my schoolteachers exhorting me and my classmates to ever greater efforts to improve our work chances, that the idea of life stages three to five became reinforced. Worse still, the educational system promoted the idea that all learning took place before reaching the age of 21, assuming you managed to get into further education. I was unable to qualify for either, I instead went into the world of horses and did my British Horse Society Assistant Instructors Certificate at age 17, as I loved riding horses and no formal qualifications were needed to get onto the course.

Luckily for me I was not talented enough to make a career in horses, and what's more, I had a desire for more from life, which as far as I could see only money could buy. Thus, I fell into life insurance sales – again, something that, back then, fortunately did not require formal qualification. It was only at this point that my curiosity began to be satisfied, as I discovered learning is something available to all. Throughout my early days in financial services, I continued to hold on to that Hollywood image of retirement, only very slowly beginning to recognise what nonsense it was. By the mid 1990's, it was evident that, whilst my clients would find later life difficult without money, they would also struggle to enjoy life without meaning and purpose to their lives.

The current convention of retirement is nothing short of ridiculous, as is the idea of fixed life stages. Patently, there are things we can only do when we are younger, for example being a professional athlete. Equally, there are many things that can only be done well with maturity and experience, such as coaching in all its forms.

All past preparation in our society has been geared towards the convention of moving from education to career, and on to retirement. We must forget all this in order to make the most of what life has to offer.

CHAPTER TWO
THE END OF RETIREMENT

I am a strong believer that retirement has long passed its usefulness to society.

Conceived in the 19th Century in Germany, the idea caught on around the world and by the middle of the 20th Century had become a lifestyle convention.

The word retirement is an awful word in and of itself. After all, this is the same word used to describe machines that are taken out of service and sent to the scrap heap. Arguably we misuse the word in any case. The word retire comes from the French "retier", which means to withdraw to a place of seclusion or safety and has its origins, as a word, in the mid 16th century. Is this a term you really want to associate with your own life?

Sadly, the word has become so entrenched in our language and everyday life that trying to eradicate it is going to take time. Let's make a start by acknowledging that retirement does not serve one single purpose in your life. I will come back to this point later, but for now just accept this as fact.

As with the mindset created by accepting life stages, taking on the mindset of retirement means we inevitably become disengaged from life. This in turn is a guarantee that later life will be miserable and shorter than it might otherwise have been.

Some of the happiest and healthiest people I know are those who continue to work and remain physically active well beyond an age when they are supposed to have retired.

The suggestion that people should never retire at first elicits a fairly negative response. I think this is because most people assume not retiring means doing exactly what they do now. This is not necessary – in many cases it won't even be possible, as the pace at which the world is changing is such that we need to continually reinvent ourselves.

For younger people, growing up in a world of constant change enables them to learn how to develop chameleon-like behaviours. It is older people who find this more challenging. Whilst humans like to stick to what they know, we live today in a society where the only constant is change. Whether you like it or not, change is all around us.

The fact that the pace of change is accelerating should not shock us. In his excellent 1989 book The Age of Unreason, author Charles Handy masterfully articulated what we are going through. In brief, Handy draws our attention to the way changes in society and business are taking place. Change, he argues, is now a constant.

One of the great changes we are experiencing is how major corporations operate. The disruption of older ways of operating will continue to impact our work, and the way we see work and working. I have never liked the term "disruption" – my first encounter with it in business was many years ago when talking to a group of venture capitalists on behalf of a client. They threw the term around looking pleased with themselves, I assume because they wanted to demonstrate they were fully up to speed with the latest business buzz words. I was really uncomfortable with the way they used the term, because it represented an adherence to "business speak". Often, terms that find their way into everyday use are picked up by us subconsciously, and in order to fit in we start using them without necessarily thinking about what they mean.

All business innovation comes about as a result of someone creating a new way of doing things. Therefore, it could be argued that if you innovate, you are by definition altering or "disrupting" another, more mature enterprise or way of doing things. This is a good thing, as it so often leads to advances and improvement. However, simply taking the word "disruption" and using it to describe what and who you are is not a good thing. Hooligans disrupt. Terrorists disrupt. Innovation and development, on the other hand, are positive terms.

What has this to do with ridding the world of retirement?

Essentially, as businesses are forced into change by competition and innovation, so the nature of their workforces will change. People will no longer have jobs for tens of years, let alone life. Some might be able to remain with the same employer by re-inventing themselves and developing new skills, but many won't and will have to move elsewhere. The long term future of company-sponsored retirement benefits does not look great – certainly joint arrangements between employer and employee to fund a retirement plan of some description may be with us for some time, but gold-plated defined benefit pensions are dead.

So too is the notion of statutory retirement ages. With this comes opportunity for older workers to continue in gainful employment, and some of that employment may come from them joining the "gig economy". Fear of this new system is misplaced, and the only people who really don't approve are the trade unions that see a loss of members and fees. To older workers wanting to achieve a healthy balance between work and play, the gig economy is a godsend.

Our ability to re-invent ourselves within the companies we work for is a phenomenal opportunity for employer and employee alike. Successful reinvention will ensure both parties continue to thrive. We need to be ready for change.

If we accept change as a constant and our roles within our own lives as a lifelong transition, then it becomes much easier to get our minds around the idea of never retiring. Life is simply what happens between the bookends of birth and death.

The economy

Uninventing retirement in the western world may prove to be a lifesaver, not just for the people who embrace this idea, but also the economy. Throughout the West there is a major pensions crisis – whether this is Government or employer-sponsored schemes does not really matter, all are in trouble. The solution that is being tried and fervently resisted is to raise the age at which people can draw their benefits.

Arguably, much of the resistance comes from a mindset of entitlement. In the UK, the idea that the state will provide something for nothing has become entrenched. Much of this thinking owes itself to the creation of the welfare state, or rather the way the origins of it have come to be understood. In the book The R Word, Time to Retire Retirement, I referenced Sir William Beveridge's report, in particular his desire to attack want. I described the promises made as idiotic, albeit those promises were made without the crystal ball that would have been needed to see the extent to which society, medicine and life expectancy was going to change. Had this been possible, perhaps the original goal might have been rowed back a little. A closer look at page three of the report (it's available on the National Archive) will reveal the following paragraph:

Social Security as envisaged in this Report is pre-eminently not a plan "for giving to everybody something for nothing and without trouble." It is a plan to secure to each citizen an income adequate to satisfy a natural minimum standard "on condition of service and contribution and in order to make and keep men fit for service."

As you can see from this brief extract it was never Beveridge's intention to provide money for nothing, and yet to increasingly many in society this is what the welfare state has come to represent. Many Baby Boomers, who were adversely impacted by changes to pensions age are of course furious at having had an expectation of benefit altered, often stating that they have "paid in" for years. Whilst at one level the Boomers indignation may be understandable, it is perhaps the over reliance on the system and misunderstanding of what the welfare state is about that is really to blame. It could be argued that successive Governments have allowed this misunderstanding to develop, it may even be that the State pension system was the very first pensions mis-selling scandal.

What is really wrong at the heart of this dilemma is the mindset that the existence of the welfare state creates. It is this very mindset of entitlement and expectation that needs to be challenged and changed.

Sadly, in the UK several generations have grown up with the idea that they "paid in, so now they should draw out", however the reality is they have done no such thing. National Insurance (tax by any other name), whilst envisaged as a means to create a fund into which people paid in order at some point in time to be able to draw on a range of benefits, this so-called fund did not really exist, as once contributions were collected by the state they were simply paid straight out to fund the benefits being claimed. Arguably the solution to the funding crisis is to call time on the state pension. I doubt this idea will catch on anytime soon.

Clearly, the underprivileged will always have to be helped, however the solution for the majority is to eliminate our own need for the state pension. If we can do this by changing our mindset, we may even persuade politicians to be honest about National Insurance, call it tax and be done with it.

Age

I suspect much of the current retirement mindset is linked to our attitude to age. Society uses age as a means to define us. Whilst there might be some logic to making sure young children do not partake in dangerous activities or that mature adults do not take part in overly strenuous sports events, this does not mean our entire lives should be dictated by our age. Yet this seems to be the case.

Our mindsets are also very often contradictory, for example we see no problem with a thirty-something athlete "retiring" from sport and then taking up a second career, but we are freaked out by the notion of a seventy-year-old job applicant. It need not be so. Our ability and willingness to do something is a far more sensible way to measure things.

Alongside an older person's ability and willingness to do things must also come the desire. Here the trouble really starts for people of a more mature age. After years of mental preparation, conditioning and the expectation of sailing off into the sunset to enjoy retirement, it can be hard to persuade a fifty-something to ditch the idea of retiring at sixty and instead continue working. It is often easier to have them acknowledge that doing something active is beneficial, but even here many only pay lip service to the idea.

By contrast, countless research studies have shown that those who have retired after a period of enjoyment lasting anywhere from a few weeks to several years, leaves many retirees with the regret of not having had a plan for their retirement. A feeling of loss accompanies retirement and for some this can be overwhelming, adding to the risks of depression and poor lifestyle choices.

Prolific business coach Dan Sullivan sets out the concept that entrepreneurs are seeking two kinds of freedom; freedom from something, and also freedom to something. The same thinking needs to apply to retiring, if we retire from something, we must aim to retire to something. This does not mean the living room couch and the television remote.

A big influence on my thinking about retirement is author, speaker and thinker Doctor Nancy Schlossberg. Dr. Schlossberg was once professor of counselling psychology at Maryland University. After retiring at the age of 69 she found life a struggle, something by her own admission she was shocked by. Despite her background, this new existence caught her by surprise, and to solve the problem she went back to work. Today she continues her work on the subject of retirement, with no sign of stopping. Nancy Schlossberg is 90 years of age.

Sadly, it is not only our mental health that is at risk – in a briefing paper on obesity to the UK Parliament published in August 2019 by Carl Baker he notes statistics for the age range 65 to 74 in which only 24 percent of people have normal weight, whilst 33 percent in this section of the population are obese. The statistics improve slightly for the over 75's. I am not sure if this is because the message starts to get through by then, or if people are dying from poor health and therefore fall out of the data. Either way this all makes for grim reading. More to the point of this book, it shows how misunderstood life beyond work has been for the Baby Boomer generation.

Preparing to move on

Although increasingly more and more people see retirement as something to avoid or defer, or at least they want to, it is also apparent many do not know how to, what they might do instead, and what steps they can take to make a successful transition into the next phase in their lives. Life is a series of constant changes, yet our lives and especially our workplaces are set up to aid development and growth through our careers, and do nothing to aid the process of leaving or changing our roles as we approach the age of retirement.

The process of preparation for retirement needs to begin much earlier than we might at first believe. When I presented my workshop program to the Human Resource team at one of the UK's largest businesses, they loved what they heard. After a pilot workshop for pre-retirees, they asked if we could provide the same for younger people. At first, I was a bit surprised and wondered at the rationale, despite my own attitude to the concepts, which just goes to show deeply ingrained these mindsets are. No one is 100 percent perfect. I agreed to a second pilot, and the company brought a couple of young people along – not only were they completely engaged in the topic, they provided some of the most engaged, helpful feedback.

The conclusion we reached after the pilots was that the workshop program needed to have phases for different ages. Not so much to prepare people for retirement, but to change the long-held mindset of retiring.

One thinker and leader in the area of ageing and its impact, is Doctor Ken Dychtwald of Age Wave. He believes there are five stages to what he calls the "retirement transition curve". I won't run through them all, however the last two are reorientation, which takes place from years 2 to 15 after retiring; and reconciliation, which occurs more than 15 years after retirement. These ideas might have some academic merit to the extent they offer an explanation of what is happening to people's minds during this time frame, but as a general way of thinking I suggest they are quite dangerous. Do you really want to spend 15 years getting your head around a life change? Imagine being 70 when you retire and then only deciding what you would like to do next at the age of 85. This strikes me as misguided.

In terms of how you think through your life, reconciliation is a potentially dangerous mindset. Certainly, it is useful to help people who have suffered a personal or physical tragedy – reconciliation is enables us to let go and move on. If reconciliation is to serve a purpose as we age, then it is of more help to reconcile ourselves to the fact that as we live, so we age. After all, the alternative to getting older is not very appealing.

It would help us far more in later life if we did not have to devote time to thinking about and rearranging our lives to adjust to being older. If we simply see later life as part of a continuum, then planning, and planning early, not only becomes essential but gets easier as we develop the habit of reviewing where we are.

Planning

During my time as a financial advisor, I spent countless hours with senior executives of large companies and entrepreneur business owners discussing their plans. None would want to run their enterprise without having some sort of business plan and strategy, yet these same people have no plan for life after work. Being too busy working might be a reasonable excuse to some degree, however the real problem lies in the way we see our lives, which is that business and work is something we do between two sets of ages: mid-twenties to mid-sixties. This makes no sense in the 21st Century, if it ever did.

Among comments made online to an article published by Harvard Business School one former senior executive posted the following:

As an executive in corporate America, I enjoyed the challenges of setting aggressive and innovative strategies and then developing the plan to accomplish or exceed the goals. For type A personalities, retirement sort of sets us adrift with nothing to fill the void. Even with hobbies and family to spend more time with, I think that I will always miss the relationships that I developed at work and the ability to mentor and develop new leaders of the future. **Harvard Business School, Welcome to retirement. Who am I now? by Dina Gerdeman**

Change is something humans struggle with – a problem that affects people from all walks of life. The challenges of life do not just affect us at retirement, we can find the same issue arise in many different areas of our lives. One person may find a change in career very easy whilst another finds it difficult, but those same two people might have the opposite reaction when it comes to moving house. The impact of change can be hard to predict. Indeed the impact of a transition may not manifest for some time, which perhaps helps to explain why so many retirees start out very happy in their new life, only to find after a matter of months that this life is not all they had hoped it would be.

Having been educated to believe that the working life takes place between the ages of 20 to 65, we have also come to believe that retirement has its set place. It is as if we see retirement as a right of passage. This right presents so many challenges it seems almost mad to want to go through it, but denying the right disturbs our equilibrium. Essentially, we don't cope with change very well.

This issue is cultural and can be seen throughout society. Our legislators and businesses adhere to the cultural convention just as rigidly, which of course they would do, as they are run by people educated to see the world this way.

Business might yet come to the rescue, in the sense of helping to lead change, by employing greater numbers of older workers. There is a certain irony in this, as business is constantly being accused of ageism. Or rather, the people that run businesses have allowed them to become institutionally ageist.

Dispensing with older workers in a world that is changing so rapidly could well be foolhardy. Although we need young, fresh talent to bring new ideas and maximise the use of modern technology, large parts of our economy have bigger, older businesses with legacy systems, products and services that require those with specific knowledge to manage, operate or run them. This may well be a short-term challenge, as the machines, processes and technology of previous generations are phased out. However, it is going to be a continuing cycle – the only difference is that the cycle will shorten and in time the technology will replace itself.

There is of course good news when it comes to change in business, in so far as once something negative starts to impact the bottom line of a company and enforced change will quickly follow. Hot on the heels of negative change you can be sure that anything that can help improve the bottom line will be seized with equal speed. Older workers could well present just such an opportunity for many businesses.

Adjustment to this rapid change, and our mindset to retirement, will require changes not only to how we see the world of work, but how we see the whole of our lives. Just as our ancestors feared the huge changes in the First Industrial Revolution, so fear of change will once again come to the fore in the Fourth Industrial Revolution.

During my lifetime, fear of change caused strife during the 1970's and 80's as skilled workers, in particular in heavy industry and manufacturing, faced a huge threat to their livelihoods as the economies of Britain and much of the West moved from a base of heavy industry to a more service-lead economy. Similar fears are being expressed today as artificial intelligence and robotics replace roles undertaken by humans. To prosper, we not only need to accept change but find ways to use our other skills, ie. those we have not used at work before, to create new careers or opportunities for ourselves. What seems certain is that coaching in its various forms will become increasingly important in the world. Therefore those able to use things such as their communication, emotional and social skills will find increasing opportunity. As demand for coaching and mentoring will increase so will the opportunity to work for oneself – an opportunity that is tailormade for those wanting to transition from full-time work to a more flexible lifestyle.

The trick to making this happen is to avoid the type of fear and mindset that befell our ancestors during the First Industrial Revolution and again in the 1980's. Protests and trades unions called for improved pay and conditions, which were indescribably bad, and many movements sought to derail change itself, as people feared for their jobs and ways of life.

If we allow a similar fixed mindset to control our views of later life and retirement, then we might well find ourselves on Dr. Dychtwald's transition curve. If we know that age changes us, and accept and continually plan for change, then we can ensure we do not waste time adjusting as we go along. We spend enough of our lives asleep and stuck in traffic to start throwing away the most valuable commodity of all whilst wondering about the new state of life we're in.

Humans struggle with change, we all do. It is often uncomfortable, scary even. This is nothing new, as we are hardwired to survive – the survival instinct triggered by a threat as seen by the Tolpuddle Martyrs is a natural reaction. However, resisting change is of little use in a fast-moving, ever-changing society. The only thing we can realistically do is accept change as part of modern life and learn the skills needed to evolve more rapidly than our ancestors.

This brings us neatly back to mindsets once more. A lot of the struggle with retirement and ageing generally stems from a fixed mindset that we were brought up and educated to accept. Whilst planning to have a more productive later life may require a different mindset, this in itself will not be enough. In fact, we must learn to adopt a changing mindset – our attitude to later life as with any other age will require us to continue adjusting.

As the world of work and business changes dynamically, it is doing so against a backdrop of very different demographics to those of the past. Life expectancy is rising, and in the developed world the birth rate has been declining for some time, so we have reached a near crisis point in respect to state-sponsored retirement plans. Put simply, there are too few people in work contributing to the system to support the growing numbers of those drawing out. This simple mathematic formula is also impacting company sponsored benefits.

Governments around the world are seeking to reflect demographic changes in state pension provision by increasing the age at which pensions can be drawn. Clearly from a financial point of view this makes sense, however the change is being resisted by the people it is most immediately affecting. For those with an expectation of ceasing work and retiring at a given age the changes are a betrayal of their "rights" and their expectations. Whist this may be understandable, I would argue that these essential changes are actually an opportunity, not a threat, in so far as they are being presented with the chance to rethink their future. This may not be a welcome chance, but in time it could be seen as the chance to properly plan for life after work rather than just stumbling into a new phase of life because that is what was expected.

We must also recognise that we are living longer, so we must accept that society simply cannot afford what it cannot afford. Secondly, using the state pension, and the age at which it is due, as a target to change how you live is a mistake – why would you allow someone else to dictate when and how you make changes in later life?

There is growing evidence that retirement is bad for our health. The statistics quoted earlier for the number of obese people is a clear indication that we give far too little thought to our health. Set against this, we also know that continuing to have meaning and purpose in our lives is beneficial for our health and welfare.

Ensuring we are both mentally and physically active provides the best chance of enjoying a healthier later life. If we add to this a growing desire for employers to retain older workers for longer, there is the potential for a win-win outcome. Even if continuing to work in your current role has no appeal, there are plenty of other opportunities for continuing work, and where remuneration is not the most critical need there are plenty of charity and volunteer options.

As we progress through early adulthood and begin to build a career, get married and start a family, it is all too easy to become wrapped up in the necessities of daily life. We are so busy working in our lives that we spend little or no time working on our lives. When life happens to us rather than the other way around, it can become deeply frustrating, particularly if at the same time you have a great idea for a new business or career, often not taking steps to pursue this idea for fear of ruining the family home. Clearly this is not true for all of us, as many people will sacrifice their home lives to succeed in their chosen career. Historically, this has tended to be men who behave this way.

Gender differences also seem to play out in terms of attitudes to changing direction once young children have grown up or left home. Women appear more patient and are prepared to wait for this moment to pursue the idea that has been brewing in their minds for some time. They take the opportunity and sense of freedom that being released from their full-time caring duties provides. Some men on the other hand, become frustrated, almost embittered, that for many years they could not, or did not, pursue their idea in order not to cause harm to the family if their venture were to fail. Over time, this can turn to anger, and a mindset becomes fixed that it is now too late. They move into retirement dissatisfied with their lives and become increasingly grumpy as they age. Why give up on that dream? Who says it is too late?

Although it is not the most exhaustive study, I can reflect on the financial planning clients I have worked with over many years, and see this play out. Interestingly, among the men for whom this has not been true, a good number found their way into entrepreneurship by accident. Being made redundant from a big company in your late forties, with children and a mortgage, is a life changing event for many. I have known some for whom this was the best thing that ever happened to them. Their experiences have all been subtly different, but once over the shock, then the struggle of the first couple of years to get established, they found themselves in a world of new-found freedom and greater choice. Choices such as who to work with, when and where.

We must recognize that there are genuine reasons why it might not be possible to quit your job and start a new venture. Many risks will be real, not imagined. Also if the idea you're passionate about is also in an area where the financial rewards may not be that great, it is clearly not wise to jeopardise the family to chase the dream. However, there is nothing to stop you making plans for the future or even starting your new venture in your spare time, working on a small scale until you are able to move on permanently.

Once again, it is apparent that it is our mindset that matters most.

It does not mean you have to work

It would be easy to infer that an end to retirement means we must continue to work. This is not the case, as it is merely the end of retirement as we have been brought up to understand it that must come to an end.

For some, working later in life might not be a choice, but in fact a necessity. Conversely there will be those of course who are financially independent, or as I like to call it financially free. The temptation for many is to do nothing, or at least not enough. If ceasing work also happens to coincide with the end of a very hard working life the desire to rest is understandable. What is important is to ensure that well-earned rest does not become a habit. Whilst humans were not designed to sit around and do nothing, the ease with which inertia sets in and becomes a habit is remarkable, not to mention dangerous.

Designing a new way of living is crucial to our health. Studies show that the risk of depression increases by up to 40 percent following retirement. Part of the explanation probably lies with the sense of loss felt when moving away from a role.

For many, our work is what comes to define us and how we see ourselves. Work is often a source of status conferred on us by others – it is the loss of this status that can cause so much damage. One day a someone, and the day after retirement an ex-someone. Psychologists have noted that because status and social circles are so often connected to our work, and that retiring from the role also brings with it a loss of your network, in its place will often be loneliness.

Adding to this pressure is the fact that you and your spouse might suddenly be spending a lot of time together for the first time in tens of years. A period of adjustment will also be needed to accommodate this.

Whichever camp you find yourself in, that time in our lives we have come to call retirement has changed, will continue to change and may yet cease to exist. To ensure we handle change well, especially where we have a chance to think ahead, we must begin to plan and plan early —not only to manage the change, but to continue to enjoy our lives.

CHAPTER THREE

GROWING AND LEARNING

If the definition of life stages no longer serves our everyday lives, then we must surely think differently about how we educate our young people, and how to continue this process as we age. For some time, one of the more obvious problems with the schooling system has been that the majority of teachers have never left school; that is to say teachers tend to have had no experience of life beyond the environment of the classroom, moving from being pupils, back to the classroom as teachers, via time spent as university students and in teacher training.

If we look deeper, we can see that little has changed in terms of the basic approach to schooling and the subjects taught since Victorian times – rather like the concept of retirement. It is little wonder, therefore, that mindsets and a fixed belief in life stages are so deeply entrenched.

Part of this outdated mindset is the mistaken belief that learning stops when we leave full-time education. Whilst we have seen changes aplenty in the workplace, with continuing education and professional development becoming part of everyday work, we do not see continued learning so much in later life, despite a proliferation of opportunity, for example The Open University or the University of the Third Age. It is not a lack of opportunity that causes us to stop learning and growing, but an attitude of mind. Change this and we can change everything.

To an extent this attitude is reinforced by the status bestowed on us by gaining professional qualifications. It is quite right we should celebrate the success of high level qualification, however our careers should not end up being based on one year of experience repeated twenty, thirty or forty times, as is sometimes the case for someone who achieves a high-level qualification during their career. It is almost as though it is the attainment, or perhaps more likely the celebration, of the award organized by others, that causes people to assume they have "made it". This might once have been the case, but can no longer be said to be true. In fact each improvement in our lives, each completed learning, is just the start of a new exciting development.

It seems to be part of the human condition that we struggle with the loss of things past. Nostalgia often overwhelms us. Recently whilst driving the young children of a friend, I pointed out a pristine example of a Triumph TR4 sportscar. They were fascinated by two things: first, how come I was so old I could remember the car, but more significant was the question, "why do people want old cars?"

Why indeed? My answer was simply that many of us, especially as we grow older, crave the comfort and memory of something that represented an important point in our lives. This tends to be something from an influential moment in our past, typically a time between our teenage years and early twenties. This may have even been part of our desire to deny ageing – a desperate urge to remain forever young. There is a significant difference between striving to remain fit and healthy for as long as we can, and simply behaving like we are teenagers once more. I am often bemused by overweight men in their middle years wearing clothing more suited to their teenage children. To my eye at least, there is nothing that ages us more than attempting to appear much younger than we really are.

One of the children asked me what the car was like. I have never driven a TR4, although I have driven cars of not dissimilar vintage, and once owned an MGB Roadster. After I had finished describing the smell of fuel, uncomfortable seats, inefficient heating, lack of air conditioning and manual wind-up windows, they were all horrified. I suggested they do their best to log the memory of our conversation, and in particular my remark that one day they too would look back fondly at something from their teenage years, and either mourn its demise or seek to recreate the memory in the way the owner of the TR4 had. I am not sure they believed me any more than I believed my elders when I was their age. There is nothing wrong with having affection for older things, or collecting them, however we must avoid allowing them to determine how we see the world. Wanting to preserve old things whilst seeking to continue to grow and learn is quite different from fighting to avoid ageing.

I plan to be around when my friend's children reach an age where they become nostalgic for something from their teens, and I fully intend to remind them about the TR4. Later, on the same day, one of the boys brought me something he had found gathering dust in his auntie's house. He handed it to me and asked me what it was. I recognized the small device instantly: it was a Nintendo DS game machine from around 2009, so only ten years old. Whilst Nintendo still make the Gameboy, youngsters mostly seem to use a mobile telephone for gaming. One day these same children may well pine for the iPhone.

I cannot speak for anyone else, but I have plenty of nostalgic thoughts. Nostalgia can also cause us to regret – in my case that I never flew on Concorde. It had been a dream of mine for years, a dream I could not afford to fulfil. Just as she was taken out of service, so my own fortunes had turned a corner and affordability to fly on Concorde to New York became a reality. Sadly, it was not to be. Whilst I still daydream about this and wish I had been able to fly, I am also well aware that regrets can be a very negative mindset. Moving on, however, is much easier said than done. One way to overcome this is to reframe our experiences. For me the way to eliminate regret is to think about flying in space.

We must learn to balance our nostalgic thoughts with a desire to remain current and stay in the present. Change, whether we like it or not, is happening, and the pace of the technological change all around us is nothing short of startling.

It is common for people to not only have nostalgic thoughts but indeed to live in the past, often to such an extent they become both disheartened by the present and miserable about the future. Yet today we live at a time where technological development is so rapid that we could be within 20 years of solving ageing and the elimination of disease.

If instead of worrying about the future through the prism of the past we flip our thoughts to the positive aspects of change, and think about the opportunities to come, it is clear to see that life has much more to be excited about than the past has to be pined for.

We are close to an age when space travel will become a regular occurrence, and medicine will improve the quality of our lives like never before. Although humans may have been responsible for considerable damage to the planet, those who develop new technologies are at the forefront of slowing, or even reversing, that damage.

How we balance our thinking between taking valuable lessons from the past, and thinking about our future, is not easy. At the extremes, we can find people who live only for the future and those who are stuck firmly in the past. I think it is important to recognise that these mindsets exist. It is also crucial to be aware that life takes place in the present – we cannot live in either the past or the future.

One of the most effective ways to overcome lapses into backward thinking is to continue learning, exploring new opportunities and developing new skills.

If you are struggling to imagine a different future, what you might enjoy learning, or skills you might like to develop (don't worry you are not alone in this), try reflecting on things you have enjoyed in the past. Then think about things you have always wanted to do but for whatever reason you have not yet done. Make a list if necessary.

Once you've made a note, sit back and imagine you have just learned that the world will end tomorrow – what have you not done that you would most like to have done? What will you miss the most?

These things will help provide you with clues as to the direction your continued growth and learning might take.

It is quite possible that you may have to try several things before you settle on what is best for you. For some people, volume of opportunities and variety are what they crave.

Whatever you do it is important to work *on* your life not *in* it.

CHAPTER FOUR

STAYING HEALTHY

On a recent trip to Toronto I had an opportunity to meet with an acquaintance who lives in Utah. He is something of an outdoors man who enjoys nothing more than hiking and running in the Grand Canyon. His are not ordinary strolls – he likes to partake in rim-to-rim hikes: essentially starting at the top of one side of the canyon, descending 6,000 feet to the canyon floor, and going up the other side. This can cover 23 miles and is often done in 100 degree heat. Each hike takes around 11 hours to complete. He even reversed the trip on a recent expedition. He looks like a man in his late forties, in fact he's 71.

A long-term client of mine, aged 82, continues to row most days of the week, and is a multiple medalist in age-related competitions. He is most often found competing against the over fifties – competitors who are often 30 years his junior.

Whilst we might not all be able to aspire to these feats, they serve as a demonstration of what could be possible. In order to remain healthy in later life, it is not necessary to go through the endeavors, of these individuals, however we do need, and must for our own sake, make efforts to keep ourselves as physically fit as possible. Improved physical fitness will not only improve our chances of good health but will also greatly enhance the chances of remaining mentally sharp. Mental health can have a serious impact on your physical wellbeing.

As with the previous chapter, it is not always straightforward to get into physical shape, especially if you have neglected exercise for some time. As with any change in life it is essential to be honest with yourself to begin with. What shape are you in? What is possible for you?

If you're not sure, then seeking advice about your physical condition is of course sensible, and a trip to the doctor might be in order before you undertake any change to your exercise routine. Also, beware of the internet if you are looking for guidance on weight loss or the right amount of exercise to take. Unfortunately, the internet is not only an excellent way to access trusted sites, for example the NHS, it is also a source of unregulated advice, opinion and untested or researched concepts, diets and health advice.

At the core of remaining healthy as we age, is what we choose to consume, and the volume of exercise we take. One basic fact is important to remember, and whilst it might sound trite, it is shocking how many people seem to ignore it: if you consume more calories than you burn then you will gain weight. Weight, as we know, is a crucial part of being healthy – weighing too little is as bad for you as weighing too much.

By 'diet', we mean what we do eat as opposed to what we do not. Rather like the word retirement, the word diet is often used in the wrong way, or at least the very mention of the word conjures up images of the need to lose weight. The word diet describes the food and liquid you consume – a restricted diet is what you do to achieve rapid weight loss. However, be aware that weight gain may simply be down to not taking enough exercise, not simply eating too much. Interestingly, one of the elements of the concept of *Ikigai* is "don't fill your stomach". *Ikigai* encourages people to eat a little less than our hunger demands.

As a young man I was extremely fit, from a combination of sports. Whilst I stopped participating in my mid-thirties, I managed to maintain fitness through riding and working with horses, something I had attempted to make a profession of when I first left school. Working all day around horses, and riding up to five a day, is a good way to maintain your fitness. However, the courage required can become difficult to maintain with age, especially if you lose motivation to overcome your fears. By the time I reached my mid-forties, my riding courage had begun to wane. Add in the increasing demands of work I started to gain weight and was getting increasingly out of shape. I managed to keep up some simple things, such as walking everywhere I could, taking the stairs and carrying my shopping around rather than using a trolley. Nevertheless, within a few short years I was not in the best of shape, or at least the shape I wanted to be in. I was also under enormous amounts of personal stress. Pressure was not that new, but my late wife's diagnosis with cancer was.

For the first couple of years of her treatment, I just got on with things and certainly paid no real attention to myself. That was until I was diagnosed with mild depression. With an occasional visit to a psychologist and a prescription of anti-depressants, I assumed all would be sorted – that is, until the drug's side effects kicked in, which were not pleasant. I discussed these with my doctor who recommended a change in drug, but I was so spooked I never took the new one. Six months later, on another visit to the GP, I saw a different doctor. Along with depression, I also had raised blood pressure and cholesterol. The doctor suggested we give mother nature a go before a review to see if it was really necessary to medicate.

The first step was exercise. I found it hard to get going – I began using a rowing machine at home and could only complete a few minutes at any one time. I stepped up my walking and cut down my alcohol intake. I had already reduced it a couple of years earlier. One of the downsides of the professional world of horses is the level of alcohol consumption. I won't go into the subject, but it is excessive. A benefit of dropping the amount of booze I consumed was weight loss, as beer and wine are very calorific. Two pints of beer, and you could take on nearly 500 calories.

As exercise became easier, I joined a gym and slowly but surely my health began to improve. Sadly, during this time my wife lost her four year fight. I am sure, had I not made changes to my lifestyle during this time, I would have coped less well with her loss and moreover could have caused myself serious harm.

If you are seriously overweight and have taken no meaningful exercise for years, then joining a gym and just going for it is likely to prove dangerous. Professional advice on how to get started is essential. As mentioned, above the internet can be a seriously dangerous place to look for advice particularly with regards to health, however some excellent tools are available to get you started on the road to fitness and weight loss. One such resource in the UK is the Couch to 5k app, which has been developed by BBC Get Inspired and Public Health England's One You campaign.

The Couch to 5k app guides you through a running exercise that builds up over a nine-week period. Once completed, you will be able to run for either 30 minutes or 5 kilometres. The app uses interval training to get you going. Week One commences with a 5-minute walk, followed by a 60-second run and then 90-second walk. This is repeated eight times, so that by the end you will have run or jogged for eight minutes. The exercise is repeated three times in the first week, with a rest day between each session. When setting the app up, you can choose from a variety of celebrities to act as your trainer and keep you going, such as 1996 Olympic double-gold medalist Michael Johnson. It is also worth noting that Johnson suffered a stroke in August 2018 that left him unable to walk. One year on he was back to normal, proving that whilst illness can strike anyone, recovery is also possible.

The app can be used on a treadmill, so there's no need to run on the road if you prefer not to. Using a treadmill might also be the spur you need to join a gym. When I first used a gym over thirty years ago, I did so to aid recovery from a serious leg injury. Up until the injury I relied on hockey or squash to keep me fit, so I was a little daunted entering a gym for the first time. The place lived up to my expectations of a macho fest, with scores of mostly men appearing to be getting in shape for a bodybuilding competition. Personal trainers seemed less interested in helping you get fit, and more about how much weight you could lift and how far or fast you could run or row. Today this has gone, so if you are fearful of going, please don't be, there is nothing to be frightened of. Personal trainers today are much more interested in helping you than creating a competitive environment.

Getting into shape is not a competition – it is about looking after yourself and ensuring you are in the best possible shape to enjoy the second half of your life. I say second half, as I am assuming the average age of readers is likely to be early fifties. These days, for many, that is only halfway on the journey, not two thirds. By coincidence, this is an age when many parents start to consider how they can help their young adult children financially. I would suggest the best help you can give them is to stay fit for as long as possible to avoid being a burden.

Also, on the One You site are other great ways to help yourself with tips on cutting down alcohol, cooking and diet, quitting smoking, and ways to improve your sleep. These can all be found on the NHS website: www.nhs.uk/oneyou.

Increasing your physical exercise is just one part of the puzzle when it comes to getting into better physical shape and staying heathy. What you consume is a critical part as well.

Hectic lifestyles and the convenience of pre-prepared food can often lead to the wrong level of calorie intake and the wrong balance of food stuffs. We have all done it, and even when taking a different approach to balancing your life, there are occasions when a ready meal or a takeaway are the only way to eat. It's important not to make this a habit. If you are in retirement or easing into retirement, there is possibly no excuse.

Cost is often cited as a reason to eat unhealthily, which is frankly not true. Ignorance of how to use cheaper cuts of meat, or ways to prepare fresh vegetables to make them tasty is a more likely reason. Personally, I am fortunate that I enjoy cooking. I also discovered that the process of preparing a meal for two was a good way to de-stress after work. It is also true I have developed a minor obsession with cookery programs, which have helped enormously in providing tips and advice to improve my culinary skills. Not every program is a "how to" guide to fine dining!

Beyond television cookery programs there are, these days, a proliferation of cookery courses, from short half-a-day to week-long courses. These can be great ways to discover more about food, food preparation and more importantly how to make the best use of seasonal ingredients. It is surprising just how easy and satisfying (both mentally and nutritionally) producing your own meals is. What's more, the cost will often be much lower than fast food from any one of the well-known brands.

Many quick-to-prepare meals involve ingredients that make up a Mediterranean diet, which has long been known to help our physical health. What's more, sensible preparation of your shopping list, good use of leftovers, or bulk buying can drastically cut the cost of the food you buy. Some foods do freeze well – buying frozen vegetables and fruits will give you a convenient supply of the right ingredients, as they defrost very quickly.

At this point it is also worth mentioning the diet of Okinawans, where the practice if *Ikigai* is very much in favour. Their diet is balanced, and according to the official travel and tourism website Visit Okinawa Japan, the preparation of the islanders' food is as important as its content. They eat plenty of fruit and vegetables, plus fish and pork. With regards to pork it is prepared by initially parboiling the meat in order to reduce the level of fat, the aim being to remove the bad cholesterol, and increase the rate of absorption of collagen.

Learning to cook can satisfy not only your food intake but also improve your mental wellbeing as you develop new skills, which satisfies the objective of always learning.

Clearly not everyone can be a gourmet cook. Many, of course, will simply not enjoy the process, but learning a few simple dishes is good for your health, easy on the wallet, and will allow you to spend what you save on better restaurants when you do decide to eat out.

Mental Wellbeing

As this chapter has already implied, staying health is not just about your body, but about your mind as well. Looking after your body can help your mind, and vice versa. One of the sad statistics of retirement is that it increases your risk of depression by forty percent.

There are many reasons as to why this is the case. Too often in life, it is our work or career that has come to define who we are, and this can mean that as we end our career, suddenly we are no longer what we were. One day the CEO, the next an ex-CEO. This sudden loss of status can have a huge impact on us, and if you add to this the loss of social contact and purpose, the impact of a total retirement can be quite profound.

For us to enjoy life we need to have both meaning and purpose. In her book *Revitalising Retirement*, Professor Nancy Schlossberg writes of the importance of "mattering". That is to say, the extent to which we command interest and are noticed by others. Although the term mattering was coined by sociologist Morris Rosenberg, Professor Schlossberg develops it to emphasise the need to remain engaged, and to make sure we make others feel that they matter.

Remaining engaged in life rather than retreating to the sofa is essential to our welfare. Sometimes this is not as easy as it sounds, some trial and error might be required as you try out different things. Do not be disheartened if you do not immediately find or discover what you would like to spend your time doing, or what provides you with meaning and purpose. It is not uncommon for this to take time, some retirees report trying several things out, sometimes simultaneously before settling on one or two activities. Remaining open minded and patient is key to your success and emotional welfare.

Finding out what provides us with a sense of purpose can prove quite difficult, and indeed some people spend many years post retirement searching for meaning and purpose to their lives. Studies have shown the searching, and the period of adjustment after retiring, can last up to fifteen years, which is a shocking waste.

I think there is little doubt that whatever we choose to do, we will also find that over time what we do will have to change in order that we remain engaged. That is perfectly normal, and is of course something that we have experienced from a young age. However, change per se is not something humans are always comfortable with, and of course can be challenging for anyone who has spent many years pursuing the same career, following a fixed pattern of life en route to success. Habits are hard to break, and those habits we may have enjoyed in the workplace harder still. In fact, one of the most common problems associated with retirement is the loss of routine – your reason for getting up in the morning. Some people seem to be hit with this instantly, for others it takes longer, particularly if in the immediate aftermath of leaving your job you enjoy a long and well-deserved rest.

The most effective way to address these issues is to consider them well in advance. Too often, people only properly consider and plan for retirement when it is imminent. This is too late. Part of the problem stems from our acceptance of retirement as a convention, combined with the fact that humans are inherently lazy and will seek out the easiest routes in decision making. For example, creating a list of things they would like to do before they die and other poorly thought through ideas. My pet hate is "the bucket list" – why younger people want to associate their dreams and aspirations with a film about the lives of two terminally ill cancer patients is beyond me.

There are countless articles, books and websites dedicated to providing inspiration about what you might do with your time after retiring, and whilst many of the adventures and escapes are likely to be unforgettable experiences, they are also unlikely to be the next thing to which you might devote yourself. They will only provide passing satisfaction and gratification, not long-term meaning and purpose.

Earlier in the chapter I mentioned an acquaintance with a passion for hiking. He enjoys some of the best scenery in the world with his passion. However, his meaning and purpose in life come from his desire to help others, which he does through his family business and his role as a coach. Likewise, my rowing client retains a part time role working in the business he built up over many years.

For both men, remaining fit and healthy is essential – they enjoy their pastimes immensely, but it is their continued careers that provide meaning and purpose to their lives.

CHAPTER FIVE

FINDING PURPOSE

Planning for life beyond your normal retirement date is not something you can do over a glass of wine and a few glossy brochures, especially after a tough day. It requires time, time to consider your situation more fully, and away from distraction. No mobile telephones, children needing help or work emails pinging in the background.

The process of planning needs to begin with a clear understanding of where you are now. This requires you to be honest with yourself about your circumstances and aspirations. It also requires you to be honest with your spouse or partner. Both of these can be a challenge. Frankly, in my experience this is not an easy part of the process. Many people will choose to duck the issues and bury their heads in the sand. In some cases, this allows negative thoughts and fears to fester only to erupt later on, often with serious consequences.

Thinking through where you are now and planning for the future might seem straightforward, yet over many years with clients I have found the opposite to be true. To help with this, I devised a simple process which I call IDEA: Imagine, Discover, Evolve, Act TM. The purpose of this is to set your imagination free, perhaps in a way you have not since childhood.

One of the problems of adulthood is we become so consumed by career and raising families we start to over-focus our minds.

That focus often becomes narrower and narrower as we progress with our work. Largely this is an essential part of the process of a successful career, but it can act as an obstacle when thinking about life after normal retirement.

To begin with, find yourself some space and quiet. Take a sheet of paper and on one side write out a list of all the constituent parts of your current role, career or job. Do not leave anything out, however menial it might seem. When you have finished, do the same for your life at home, and perhaps your favourite pastime. Lose yourself in whatever the activity is, close your eyes if necessary, and visualise performing these roles. Write everything down, leave nothing out.

Once the lists are complete, circle each of the items you enjoy most or are best at – you may find the two are often the same. It is perfectly normal to find the things we enjoy most are also those at which we excel, and vice versa. Once finished you should have separate lists for work, home and possibly your pastimes.

Now write the words you circled and write them out in separate lists, preferably on different pieces of paper. Now, take some time to imagine other applications for each of the skills you noted. Let yourself go, use your imagination as you would have done as a child. From this list you can create another list of things you might do later in life – this process is to help you evolve to a point where you can then take action.

The chances are this is not the last time you will need to do this. You may even have to repeat it a few times in the short term as your thinking evolves and you try out new things.

As your life progresses, you may find you're no longer able – or no longer have the desire – to do whatever you have planned, at which point you can repeat the same exercise to take you to something new.

Life itself should involve continued learning; discovering there is a new activity or hobby you might like to try provides the perfect opportunity for learning. Lifelong learning is of invaluable benefit to our welfare, aside from the obvious improvements to our career prospects. A life spent absorbing new information not only ensures we keep up to date with the world, but it helps maintain our health for longer. As we live longer it clearly makes more sense for our enjoyment of this extra time, to do so as healthily as we can. If we add the word learning to the concept of IDEA™ we get IDEAL. What we are aiming for therefore is to take your IDEA™ output to help you create your IDEAL life.

IDEAL in this sense does not mean perfect. You must also be aware not to set out in pursuit of perfection. Most people would agree this is impossible, however many will assume they require the plan they have in place has to be perfect. It doesn't need to be. What's more, you probably cannot create the perfect plan, so don't even try. Simply getting started, and refining as you go, is far better than frittering away time trying to reach perfection. Whilst this is true throughout life it is especially true in retirement, as the very process of considering and imagining your new future will involve you making discoveries about yourself, discoveries that will enhance the quality of your later life. It could be argued that deciding to remain engaged with life and the world is purpose in and of itself.

The link between our health and having a purpose in life is well understood. Separating the two into different sections poses a problem for how and where to address certain aspects of both.

I wanted to separate health and purpose as whilst they are inextricably linked your purpose may change over time, it probably already has at times in your life. Retirees often report they no longer find purpose in something that had been important to them and find themselves struggling to find a new purpose. Even when we are committed to continuing review of where we are in life it is possible on occasion to find ourselves in something of a gap. When this happens, it is crucial that we remain physically active as this can and does help us combat the sense of loss that might repeat if you find you no longer have purpose.

Purpose brings meaning to our lives, physical fitness alone cannot. But being physically well provides us with a substantial boost to our mental wellbeing. Specifically, exercise causes the release of endorphins: a chemical which reacts with your brains receptors and triggers a positive feeling both in your mind and in your body. My own issues with mild depression and stress-related physical problems have been managed by regular exercise, but they have only been fully combatted when I also have purpose. We must never underestimate the impact that looking after ourselves physically can have on our mental welfare, but it is not a substitute for finding a purpose.

Just what is purpose?

There is a temptation to think our purpose needs to be something bigger and grander than ourselves: a major statement of our place in the world. The problem with this mindset is it can cause us to feel inadequate, as often the result of this thought process is to search for comparisons. Not everyone is going to make ground-breaking scientific discoveries or develop a new technology that changes the world we live in, so comparing yourself or trying to compete in this way is futile, and counterproductive to your own wellbeing.

A wonderful example of how to view the future comes from Japan. There is no direct translation of the word retirement in Japanese. There is however the term *Ikigai*, which has a number of translations, one a "Sense of Life Worth Living" basically, translates in English to "your reason for getting up in the morning" or your "reason for being".

Japan has the oldest per capita population in the world. Approximately 27 per cent of the Japanese population is over the age of 65. Outside of eastern Europe, Japan is also one of the countries with the highest density of cigarette smokers, and moreover, they work longer hours than most of the rest of the developed world. Before you wonder if I am about to suggest taking up smoking and routinely working 80 hours a week, I am not. I am, though, suggesting that having a reason for getting up in the morning is an extremely powerful mental stimulus.

One of modern life's great preoccupations is the pursuit of happiness. The idea, if taken literally, will presumably guarantee a life of unhappiness – if one is always in pursuit, one is never happy. Whilst this might be an over-simplified view, it does highlight once again the danger of our language, and it can negatively impact our daily lives and how we see the world.

Since we can neither live in the future or the past we must live in the present. This might seem obvious, however I am sure you can think of someone who is perennially preoccupied with the past and others for whom tomorrow will always their lives improve.

Although we might miss many things from the past, the past cannot be brought forward, nor can you live tomorrow without first living through today, despite a desire to be in a better place than might be the case right now. How we speak to ourselves can have a significant effect on our mental outlook. Continuing to have a meaningful present is also the means by which we can have a positive impact on others and the world at large.

If you're thinking this is easier said than done, you are quite right.

I know a little about life's challenges. I have a minor physical disability (this is a relative term), and whilst it is not visibly obvious, its causes and subsequent consequences have blighted my life. To this day I fight against the damaging negativity my condition causes me. I cannot do away with the past nor can I change the everyday effect. I am not setting this out to seek sympathy, but merely to point out that, for some people, finding purpose, and developing the mindset and habits that can help with this, is not at all straightforward. Indeed, the very effort to create the right mindset can be part of your purpose.

Over the years I have read many self-help books, attended conferences and heard hugely uplifting tales. Often the books and presentations have been delivered by people with little or no understanding of the challenges many of their readers or listeners face when trying to put these valuable messages into action. I hope by saying a little about myself I can demonstrate some level of empathy with those for whom changing mindsets and their approach to life is challenging and urge you to take the first steps. One thing that is clear about finding purpose is the task is not always straightforward – indeed, studies have found it can take many years for some people to find their purpose in retirement. My hope is to aid the process, to try to make it as easy as possible and provide the ideas for those who need to re-purpose their lives the means to do so. It is possible that you may need to find a new purpose more than once as life moves ahead.

The propensity to have simple ways to define ourselves, for example "I'm a surgeon" sadly helps to pigeon hole us. Although in recent years there has been an increase in the idea of having multiple careers, the notion of being a polymath has bypassed many in the baby boom generation by. It is simply not the case to believe that just because a career or profession has been central to our lives that we cannot now develop new skills, or find new ways to deploy existing underutilised skills. We just have to find those things that we want to do or activities in which our existing skills can be used.

There are numerous books covering the subject of *Ikigai*. Each brings something subtly different to the subject, partly I think, down to the difficulty of describing what is fundamentally an approach to living. According to Dan Buettner, author of *The Blue Zones of Happiness*, there are other parts of the world that have a form of *Ikigai*, albeit not called this. The origin of the term 'blue zones' is disputed, and I am not going to join the debate.

What we can say though is that the areas of the world described as blue zones are also places where life expectancy exceeds that of other parts of the same country in which the blue zones are located. One other example being the Italian island of Sardinia.

Clearly, we cannot all simply move to Okinawa or Sardinia, nor can we necessarily benefit from the weather experienced in each place, which is also cited as part of the reason for longevity.

For me, the real key to helping us is the attitude of mind that exists in places like Okinawa, which is a belief that sitting around doing very little is inherently bad for us. What we must take from *Ikigai* is the essence of each of the concepts and translate these as closely as possible to fit the parts of the world we each live in. We can summarise these in a simple list, which I have taken from the book *Ikigai: The Japanese secret to a long and happy life* by Hector Garcia and Francesco Morales:

- **Stay active, don't retire.** Those who give up the things they love to do, and do well, lose purpose in their lives.
- **Take it slow.** Being in a hurry is inversely proportional to quality of life.
- **Don't fill your stomach.** As mentioned earlier, eat less than your hunger demands.
- **Surround yourself with good friends.** Friends and friendship are the best medicine.
- **Get in shape for your next birthday.** Exercise releases endorphins that are so helpful to our mental welfare.
- **Smile.** A cheerful smile is not only relaxing (smiling requires fewer muscles than scowling), it also helps make new friends.

- **Reconnect with nature.** Get outdoors, whether this is by gardening or taking up hiking it doesn't matter – city living alone is not good for us.
- **Live in the moment.** We cannot live in either the past or future. Whilst we can use past experience to guide us and future plans to excite us, we must live today.
- **Follow your *Ikigai.*** In other words, follow your passion.

CHAPTER SIX

SOCIAL CONTACT AND FRIENDSHIPS

Remaining connected to others is a vital part of life, regardless of your age. However, we know that one of the biggest challenges faced by older people is loneliness. It is in fact, a killer.

Friendships can slowly ebb away over time, often unnoticed until it is too late. There are a variety of reasons for this that we will come on to, however the obvious route to combat it is to develop a habit of forming new friendships. Doing so can be more challenging if we have lost our sense of purpose in life. Having little or no purpose will often create low mood or worse, and if so, finding and making new friends becomes increasingly difficult, if not impossible.

Like physical and mental health, purpose and social contact are connected – almost to the point where one cannot exist without the other.

In smaller communities, maintaining social contact is easier than in a large town or city. I recently moved to a new city, and although fairly small, the place is large enough at around 125,000 people, with many travelling in and out for work. In such an environment it is difficult to have close contact with other residents. I am fortunate that the city has an historic centre and the characteristics of the landscape has caused the city to develop distinct districts, so there are ways to mix with those living close by.

As with anything worth achieving in life, it takes some effort to get to know people around you. This of course can be especially challenging if you are not a naturally outgoing person. The district I am in has a few small shops close by – good shopkeepers are a godsend for the naturally shy, as they will tend to get you talking even if you don't want to! So don't do all your shopping online or at the hypermarket that requires you to drive to it – take a walk to the local shops instead.

Local shops are often great places to discover other simple community based activities that might interest you, through handily posted notices and cards. Local tradespeople can also help you fit in and find new contacts. This can be daunting for the shy person, but in my experience other people are not ogres and are often very welcoming of the new kid on the block.

There are many reasons why it's good to develop the habit of making new acquaintances who may become friends. Retiring from a job is one of them.

The severing of social ties that exist in the workplace can create a sense of loss, and is often cited as an issue by the recently retired who miss regular interaction with colleagues. It can also affect those who work remotely or from home.

It is quite possible that you have taken for granted your workplace relationships over the years, and the value they bring has perhaps been ignored. This can be especially true during busy and stressful periods, as we become ever more focused on the work in hand and cease to notice the people around us – until they are no longer there. Or, more to the point, you are no longer there.

Workplace-based relationships, or rather the relationship with individuals you met or got to know through work, can of course be maintained beyond retirement. There is nothing to prevent people from meeting in social settings away from work and continuing their friendship. Sometimes this is not as easy as it sounds and can be adversely affected by the role of the recently retired, particularly if that role conveyed a level of status on the individual. Losing workplace status can impact our mental health and can also lead to strains in relationships with former colleagues, especially if the retired person is struggling to let go of the past. This is of course heightened if the working friend brings news of recent changes at the organization, and the changes are affecting the retired person's legacy. The blow to the ego must not be underestimated.

A few years ago, in a bid to improve my presentation and speaking skills, I joined a local club of Toastmasters. It was fun and introduced me to a new range of people – folk I would otherwise never have met. One thing that I found very interesting about this particular club was the number of younger people, especially immigrants to the UK. I was surprised to discover they all either worked for, or had a connection with, one of the biggest employers in the area: a multi-national telecommunications company. These young people must have had enlightened managers, as they had been encouraged to join the club to overcome shyness and improve their English. That said the young were not the only attendees, indeed many were much older than me and their continued participation was part of their social contact. One gentlemen who joined during my time was in his mid seventies. Over the time I attended the club, it was fascinating to see how these people developed and grew.

There are of course many other local and community activities we can participate in, it's just a question of looking – and taking the opportunity to try something new.

At the opening of this chapter I used the word 'connected'. Today, being connected is frequently assumed to mean being online. Unfortunately, social media, through which many of us "connect" with people, uses words like 'friend' to describe the people we are connected to. Whilst you may have online connections with friends and perhaps re-connect with old friends or acquaintances, this form of connection or friendship is not a substitute for physically meeting another person. This is not to say friendships cannot begin online – they do of course, and it can be a good way to make initial steps towards meeting new people. But ultimately it is shared companionship that serves us well and is at the heart of the positive experiences of people living in blue zones.

Making new friends can be a serious challenge for some people. The causes are various, and individual experiences will differ. The mental health charity Mind (www.mind.org.uk) provides a lot of guidance on the subject of loneliness, as well as support and an online service called Elefriends, a reference to the elephant in the room. This service may be online, but it is not a social media platform. To quote Mind directly:

"Elefriends is a supportive online community where you can be yourself. We all know what it's like to struggle sometimes, but now there's a safe place to listen, share and be heard."

The site is moderated between set hours and is operated by the charity. On the main website's pages there are useful tips to avoid or overcome loneliness, and interestingly the key messages resonate with the ten tips of *Ikigai*. In the section "Look after yourself", you will find these headlines:

- **Try to get enough sleep**
- **Think about your diet**
- **Try to do some physical activity**
- **Spend time outside**
- **Spend time with animals**
- **Avoid drugs and alcohol**

Whichever way you look at your lifestyle to get the most benefit from retirement, there is a clear connection between your lifestyle habits and your mental approach or mindset.

Friendships can end for all sorts of reasons – one which occurs frequently as we age is bereavement. Sadly, this is something else I have had personal experience with. There are some aspects of bereavement that are possibly quite obvious, the immediate sense of loss of your loved one, the strange feelings that arise around the home you once shared. Memories come flooding back when you find yourself in a particular place or at a particular time of the day. There is no apparent pattern to these things occurring. Despite having time to prepare (as I had as my wife fought her cancer) you find yourself walking into rooms expecting to see your spouse or partner there. These same feelings can occur when a relationship breaks down – something that is happening with increasing frequency to the over sixties.

What is less obvious is how other friendships can break down. During my career as a financial advisor I worked with a number of clients who chose to retire abroad. The attraction of better weather and a community of people in similar circumstances is clear. Life can be idyllic for some who choose this path – unless a partner dies.

After the initial shock and grief, the survivor can slowly find themselves feeling isolated. Invitations to parties start to slow or even dry up, and even if this does not happen the individual can feel awkward, especially if they are the sole widow or widower among a group of friends. In many cases the survivor will seek to move back to the UK to be close to family. This can prove costly, and whilst it might well provide emotional support and comfort, for example through relationships with grandchildren, it can prove just as hard to make new friends as it would have been elsewhere.

This also happens when the bulk of your friendships were established via your deceased partner. It is crucial, therefore, to ensure we have our own circle of friends and do not simply depend on our spouse's connections.

CHAPTER SEVEN

GIVING BACK

Have you ever noticed just how satisfying it is to give to others? From watching the delight of loved ones opening surprise presents to simple acts of kindness that cost nothing, we all get a boost from providing for other people.

Giving with the intent only that a gift is of value or worth to the recipient, as opposed to being driven by selfish motives, is a fruitful way to go through the day.

For some, giving back is a full-time purpose, and I am sure you can think of many examples of selfless acts of simple kindness as well as truly remarkable acts of selflessness. However, we must take care that our efforts to give are definitively about the act and the recipient, not ourselves. Whilst we can derive enormous satisfaction from helping people, and receive a sense of satisfaction, we must do so without hoping to be recognised and thanked – a desire that is all too common.

Having a sense of gratitude for ourselves and the life we have is an important part of developing our sense of self worth. Being grateful for even the minor things in life can, on its own, help to create a more generous spirit. All too often people can see what is wrong in the world, what is wrong in their lives. It is easy to look around us and see a litany of problems to solve and difficult obstacles to overcome. Doing so continually causes negative emotions and mindsets. Rarely are problems solved and challenges met by a negative mindset. On the other hand, appreciating what you have and being grateful each day leads us to see the same obstacles from a more positive perspective increasing our capability to find a solution. With this emotion at the front of our minds it becomes easier to give back.

Remaining well and healthy is a crucial part of our capacity to give to others. Interestingly, the more we give the more we tend to receive, so the interconnection between gratitude and giving creates a virtuous circle – all of which contributes to us remaining as mentally well as possible as we grow older.

Some people like to give back by taking on voluntary roles, whether as a school Governor or a local parish councilor or helping with committees of one sort or another. Clearly these are all admirable ways we can give our time to assist others, but this should not become a full-time occupation. Furthermore, it makes sense only to take on roles that fit either with your core skills or your passion.

Too often, local committees for sports clubs or the local village fete are led by the same individuals. At times, quite genuinely, there is a shortage of volunteers, and the same people find themselves being roped in. Given that one of the objects of giving is to help, assist and demonstrate gratitude it is best to avoid too much work and stress created by overinvolvement. It is inconceivable that you can go through this stage of your life without some degree of disagreement with others, so taking care to limit the number of situations in which this can occur is in your own best interests.

As I write, I am reminded of a piece of advice I read from Sir John Timpson of the eponymous shoe repair chain. When asked, in his regular Daily Telegraph business advice column, about business networking he expressed a degree of personal discomfort with such events. He went on to suggest they can be good opportunities, but also that they should not become the enquirer's full-time occupation. Although specific to the world of business, his remarks are equally appropriate in other walks of life.

One common route to giving back to our communities is to get involved in local organisations, whether that is the Parish committee or a local charity. All worthy things to do and I would not discourage getting involved. However, I would also urge that care is taken not to turn this into a full time lifelong commitment, much like Sir John's observations concerning networking. Obviously, all these causes are crying out for volunteers, however all too often the same faces are found in all of them. Any organization whether a large business or local club do benefit from a change of guard on a regular basis, new blood with fresh ideas. It can become a trap if we are not careful.

Being around new people and developing new relationships can sometimes be a challenge especially as we age, the discomfort we feel with changes is often magnified, however embracing change and moving on or welcoming new faces into our world is healthy for our minds. Healthy minds are a positive, almost imperative element of being healthy in the round.

I would go further and suggest avoiding committees that seem to have the same people present as all the others in your area.

If you find this to be the case, maybe step away and seek other ways to give back. One last point about Sir John, he and his late wife Lady Alex fostered 90 children during their lives together. That is a lot of giving.

If committees are not for you, there are plenty of other community-based activities that enable you to give back. Among these are local groups dedicated to transporting the unwell and elderly to and from hospital appointments. Being old and ill is no fun – being old, ill and alone is far worse. The extra comfort provided by having someone with you during these times cannot be overstated.

One area with growing demand is cancer support. In my local area, as well as services provided by the NHS and well-established charities such as Macmillan, we have a local group dedicated to transporting patients to and from hospitals for treatment. Having to go through chemotherapy is a mental and emotional challenge that only those who have had the misfortune to experience it can fully understand. As a carer in the past, I have some sense of the trauma (the loved one's journey has its own specific horrors) experienced by the patient. The jangling nerves on the way to hospital for the first treatment are swiftly followed by collapse. Tears usually overwhelm stoicism. Depending on the course of treatment and the individual, the second or third visit is usually when the dread truly kicks in. The hours spent hooked to a machine listening to its constant beeps, with a small alarm going off as each drip bag empties, makes the pressure most of us worry about at work seem like a walk in the park. Worse, though, is the anticipation of the side effects: the sometimes violent sickness, terrible raised temperatures, breathing difficulties and, as happened with my late wife, emergency readmission to cope with these side effects. Now imagine doing all of that alone.

Clearly a volunteer driver is not going to able to be with the patient 24/7, but simply having someone to talk to as they are taken to hospital, and whilst they are connected to that infernal machine, is of more comfort than I can express. For the volunteer, these can be energy sapping and emotional days – doing this is not for everyone, nor I suspect is it a good idea to do too much or for too long. After all, we also must look after ourselves.

Taking care of ourselves is one of the best gifts we can ever give. By needing less healthcare or support we make less demand on the system, in turn creating space for others. This may be an unrewarded gift, but then why do any of this for reward? Giving is primarily to aid the recipient, but it is also a satisfying and life-enhancing act for yourself. It can, and does, provide both meaning and purpose.

If assisting people with transport is not for you, there are a host of other things such as helping in the pop-up shops local charities often have at hospitals, taking tea and cakes into the wards or using your technology skills to help sell second-hand items collected by other volunteers. One local group close to me are constantly looking for people to manage the online sales of items.

Hospices have similar needs – my 82-year-old mother spends one day a week volunteering at her local hospice. Interestingly, her involvement with the hospice, whilst brought about by her own personal loss, has created an additional opportunity for her meet and engage with a group of people she may not have met otherwise. In addition to doing things for and on behalf of the hospice they have regular social gatherings enabling all to maintain healthy contact in the community.

CHAPTER EIGHT

KEEP WORKING

I thought long and hard about where to place this chapter, the obvious place would have been as chapter three, however I opted to put it towards the end in order not to deter readers who may either be retiring later than the norm, or who are in a role that has left them exhausted and utterly dissatisfied. Suggesting to either that they keep working when maybe all they can consider is stopping, might cause them to stop reading. My hope, of course, is that what has gone before will provide methods, ideas and maybe even a little inspiration to entertain the notion of continuing to work in some form or other.

'Keep working' does not of course mean either that you should continue in your present role or continue to work at the pace you may have done in the past. Whilst for some, continuing to play a part in their current profession may appeal, to others reaching normal retirement age is an opportunity to do something new. This is not a one-size-fits-all exercise.

Continuing work is a fulfilling way to remain engaged with the world, and with life. Working can provide meaning and purpose, which are two crucial things we require to help us to live healthier for longer. Work does not have to be remunerative either – there are plenty of charity or not-for-profit opportunities where the only recompense you might receive is a reimbursement of expenses. For those who may have a delicate financial position, this may not sound too appealing, however it is worth remembering that whilst at work we tend not to be spending, sitting around at home actually adds to household expense, through heating, electricity and eating during the day. Although not enormous sums, if you can defray your level of outgoings even for only a year or two, it is possible your existing savings may grow, or at least last a bit longer.

With the substantial increase in part-time and casual roles, it is perfectly possible to spend some time working for reward, and some time working for charity. There are no rules. We are free to create our own and develop a framework for our lives. This period is an opportunity to take back control of your time.

As referenced in a previous chapter, one element in the concept of *Ikigai* is to stay active and don't retire. Remaining active is also contained within the charity Mind's advice for avoiding loneliness. There is plenty of evidence that retiring is not that good for us and can be a cause of loneliness. As I said in the introduction, humans were simply not designed to do nothing. For previous generations, retirement as I have defined it was the only realistic option. After all, with countless years of hard, often dangerous, work behind them, they were simply too exhausted to do much else.

Today the situation is very different. Many more people in the developed world work in service-related industries, and the physical dangers of previous generations are far less common. Those still working in heavy industry have machines and robots to help them, and an environment that is carefully managed to ensure health and safety. Ironically, working in service industries still has its dangers, as it can lead to a sedentary life. Add in overeating, too much alcohol, increased levels of mental pressure and stress, and you have a recipe for poor health. Therefore the temptation not only to cease work, but never work again is obvious. However, it is important to evaluate carefully your circumstances once you have had a period of retirement. Various studies have found that people retiring early from a stressful job have better survival rates at the five year point post retirement. Partly this can be explained by having more time to be able to take care of one's health.

Part of the argument for continuing to work centres around life expectancy. Life expectancy has improved enormously. In the first few years of the 20th Century, UK life expectancy for a woman was 52 years, 48 years for a man. By the turn of the current century life expectancy at birth had extended to 83 and 80 years respectively. Statistics can be misleading, and these numbers are averages, today according to data released in September 2019 by the Office for National Statistics (ONS) a man aged 65 has approximately 18.6 years to live and a woman can expect to live a further 21 years. Approximately one quarter of these people will reach their mid 90's. Vastly different from 100 years ago.

The drive for people to retire earlier, which also comes with significant improvements in lifestyle during the late 20th century, could see someone living for thirty or even forty years in retirement. We are just not built to do this.

Although it is a small sample, I can say of all the clients I have advised who reached their early eighties none had been retired for over twenty years, several were either still working, at least part time, or active in other ways, until very close to their death. In Chapter 4, I mentioned two people I know, both of whom remain very active (I realise their level of activity may well be beyond most people), what I did not mention is they both work. To remind you, one is in his early seventies and the other is ten years older.

There are plenty of examples of people in the public eye continuing to work. In the UK we have a wonderful example of a life dedicated to work in Her Majesty The Queen, clearly not a role anyone can apply for, but something she does despite the possible option to step down. A more reasonable comparison is with people in the arts continuing to act, perform or write, such as author John Le Carre aged 87 and broadcaster Sir David Attenborough at the age of 93. Businesswoman and philanthropist Dame Shirley Stephanie is still writing and speaking at the age of 86, and an influence on my thinking who I mentioned in Chapter 4 is Professor Nancy Schlossberg, also still actively writing and speaking at the age of 90. There are many more of course, each providing inspiration of what is possible.

Whether we like it or not, we all age. Each of us lives at least part of our lives believing the normal rules don't apply to us and that somehow we will live forever. I sometimes wonder if those with questionable lifestyles – carrying a little too much weight, eating and drinking too much in their forties and fifties – continue to harbour this belief, which reminds me of one of my favourite one-liners: "denial is not just a river in Egypt." We can choose to accept the reality of ageing and the likelihood of poor health towards the end of our lives, or not. Those who do accept it and are honest with themselves, gain the chance to live healthier for longer.

Who knows, they may even ensure they live much longer as well. Sitting around doing nothing is a certain recipe for poor health. One of the flaws of modern medicine is, whilst it can help us survive, there is sometimes a high price to pay in terms of the quality of life that results. I have personal experience of a life that was endured rather than lived and enjoyed, by medicines ability to push back the date of the inevitable.

Choosing the name of this chapter was not easy. The way the future is going, I am not necessarily sure it will be the case that people will work longer, but I do know that the way we work throughout life is changing. For many years I told my clients that retirement had un-invented itself. What's also true is what we came to understand as the world of work has been un-inventing itself for a long time, as increasing use of technology, in particular artificial intelligence, is changing in the work place, these changes are set to accelerate.

One other change in work habits is the growth of the gig economy. Today, this phrase is frequently used in connection with zero-hours or short-term contracts. However, the term 'gig' has been used in the entertainment industry for years. Historically, working in the arts was seen as a lifestyle choice, and therefore the incumbent risks of not having permanent employment are assumed to have been accepted. This is a situation we may all have to get used to, the result being our working lives are extended but we may experience periods of not working or only working limited hours in between periods of longer term full time employment or work.

The controversy caused by the use of zero hours contracts, whether fixed, paid or not, in the mainstream workplace, is in danger of obscuring what is going on. I have no doubt that some people are being exploited; however, it is not my objective to get into employment law or rights issues, rather to highlight that the gig economy is here, and I believe here to stay. The result being more and more people will work in this flexible way adopting the lifestyle choice of those in the arts. This being the case it follows that retirement per se will cease to exist for many as there will simply not be the type of jobs or roles that will need to be retired from. Whilst this may sound a little disconcerting to some I see this as providing a more exciting future, one in which older people will remain engaged with wider society far more than is perhaps the case today. Time will tell.

Large, overly bureaucratic organisations are being disrupted by newer leaner organisations that operate through the gig economy. It is also increasingly popular as a way of working – I have several younger clients who work this way, such as by taking very short-term commissions for specific work or running multiple services or jobs.

Some people like choice, choosing how to work, when to work and for whom to work. As organisations fragment, support networks once found in the organisation will disappear, increasing the need to collaborate and look elsewhere for help. Self-employed tradespeople have been doing this for decades. What the gig economy provides is opportunity to use skills later in life that we might otherwise set aside.

When it comes to looking at the spread of the gig economy, all sorts of statistics abound, for example in a 2016 study into independent working by the management consultants Mckinsey & Company found that independent workers make up nearly 30% of the workforce in the USA and Europe. At the time of the study 57% of the over 65's in work in Europe were doing so on an independent basis, in the USA the figure was just under a half of those in work over age 65. The trend towards independent work is accelerating and surveys suggest there is a desire among younger age groups to work independently.

The McKinsey report and many others draw on huge amounts of data and as such it can be hard to understand precisely what is going on. That said we do seem to be entering a phase that will see a large reduction in employed workers with a corresponding increase of independent workers. Mass full time employment was a creation of industrialisation, a trend which accelerated in the first seventy years of the 20th Century, since then we have witnessed a gradual increase in self employment. In these regions at least we are seeing the tide change. Change is always challenging, in the UK politicians have voiced concern about the rise of independent working, perhaps predictably, however the points they make are based on outdated and 'old' economy thinking, whether this is those to the left expressing the view that the gig economy is simply a way to exploit people, or those to the right suggesting the rise is simply about freedom of choice. As the saying goes, they're guilty of 'analogue thinking in a digital world.'

In the USA, 51 per cent of those working in the gig economy are women, and in the UK this number rises to 57 per cent. It is easy to see why politicians on the left want to seize on these numbers, but if you dig a little deeper you will find a few fascinating things going on. In the UK, 14 per cent of those working this way are aged over 65, while in the US it is 8 per cent. The McKinsey research found that around 30 per cent of all those working this way do so out of necessity. We can make all sorts of assumptions about why and how this necessity arises, but based on my own experience of the over-65s, the necessity to continue working is self-imposed – that is to say the additional income is actually for aspirational gain, such as taking an extra holiday, running two cars rather than one or helping their children out financially. Based on the clients I have worked with over the years, most work because they want to, because they feel far from 'finished'.

The survey also showed that independent workers reported higher levels of job satisfaction than those who are employed. They enjoy greater freedom of where and when to work, they are more engaged and most importantly of all perhaps, they enjoy the opportunity to be their own boss. Satisfaction levels varied depending on whether working independently was down to choice or through necessity – though, I have worked with clients who found themselves in this situation out of necessity and while the first couple of years was a struggle, they became used to the unpredictability of work and learned how to operate a small business. The clients I advised not only thrived and enjoyed what they were doing, but in a number of cases have continued well past their normal retirement age, working as and when they choose. These reluctant entrepreneurs found that they enjoyed continuing to work.

Although in the UK it is now against the law to force older people to retire, this does not remove the deep-seated, almost sub-conscious belief that a certain age is the expected time to retire. Being told when you can and can't retire is a sure-fire way of getting the wrong reaction. What the McKinsey survey does not get into is the trend for older employed workers turning to the courts, seeking resolution to disputes over being side-lined due to their age. Many large organisations, whether through ignorance or other misplaced bias, see older employees as something they can do without and where either new roles arise or contracts require renewal instinctively seek a younger person. There have been several high profile cases involving the media industry in the UK, where older television presenters have found themselves replaced by younger ones. How long will this continue before new employees at even the most staid, established businesses are only able to work as freelancers? This trend is well underway in the UK, with large businesses laying off people around the age of 50, who in turn start up their own consultancy business, often returning to work for the employer that just made them redundant.

The process of removing people from the workforce only to take some of them back as contractors has the potential to cause long term damage to business both through the loss of skills and a simple lack of potential replacement employees caused by demographic changes.

One country grappling with demographic challenges is Japan. The Japanese Ministry of Internal Affairs and Communications found in a 2017 survey that the number of over 65's employed in large organisations had risen to over eight million, just over 12% of the total employed workforce. The prime reason for the increase was put down to worker shortage.

A further point of interest in the McKinsey survey, is that the biggest growth in the numbers of independent workers is among Millennials. Perhaps this should not be surprising – to take a quote directly from the survey: "The Industrial Revolution moved much of the workforce from self-employment to structured payroll jobs. Now the digital revolution may be creating a shift in the opposite direction." If this is correct, and there is every reason to assume it is, then old structures around retirement and the notion of what it represents are in their death throes, not just reacting to the financial circumstances of the post-credit-crunch period. In other words, retirement has un-invented itself.

In the book *The R Word: Time to Retire Retirement* I mentioned the case of a client from my financial planning business, James, although that is not his real name. At the age of 50 he was made redundant, and whilst he had seen it coming, he was nevertheless in a bad place emotionally. He also assumed he was in a poor place financially. He wasn't, or at least his long-term future and that of retirement were financially in a decent place. His sole risk was that he might have to exhaust savings and investments in the short term to finance his family. He had, however, a combination of distinct knowledge and experience in an area of his profession that was also going through an increase in demand due to regulatory changes. All he needed to do was harness that experience and present his credentials to the right people. It was not easy to persuade him that this might be possible, but he quickly learned that he would struggle to find a job despite his qualifications as would-be employers were all seeking younger people. Silly them.

Having set himself up as a consultant and by tapping into his professional network, he slowly but surely "gigged" his way to a viable business that not only erased his emotional fears, but also ensured confidence in his family finances. This was over 12 years ago – now on the cusp of his 63rd birthday and with his wife pursuing a passion which provides her with both meaning and purpose, he plans to continue to work. Over the last 3 years he has allowed the contracts he takes on to reduce in volume, meaning he no longer needs to bring in extra people to help him. He has also created time to start exploring other options in life, taking up long-forgotten hobbies and involving himself in local community issues. We will continue to review his plans over the coming years as he considers where he sees himself in the future. Not needing to suddenly stop work has been enormously beneficial. Not only has it helped stave off the sense of loss that a cliff-edge retirement can bring, it has afforded him time to experiment with other options without any pressure.

Changes in the way the economy works are of enormous benefit to a longer working life, as businesses need to have more fluid workforces to meet the challenges of constant change driven by technology, so it is likely that demand for independent workers will increase. In turn many periods of work may be short term in nature, which may be idea for the older worker no long seeking full time employment. This may also lead to an increase in multiple "employments", or a portfolio of roles.

As technology has enabled substantive changes to our everyday workplaces. The temptation to work from home is enormous, however if you have spent most or all of your working life in a collegiate environment then suddenly working alone can present considerable challenges, not least of which is the loss of social contact and therefore an increased risk of loneliness. One way to combat this is to work from elsewhere occasionally – this could be from a local coffee shop or a local serviced office hub where hot-desking facilities can be very good value for money. Each of us likes to work differently, so finding the right balance might take a bit of trial and error.

Along with the loss of social contact through the workplace, some people find they miss "going to work" – maybe not the commute on packed trains or driving in the rush hour (we need a new name for this too, when did you last rush?), but the daily routine of getting up, getting ready and leaving home to go to work. I found this hard to come to terms with.

After the death of my wife, I moved away from the area I had lived in for many years, which involved a much longer drive to the office. Typically, I commuted to London by train one day a week for many years, so I was at least used to working in different locations. Following the move my solution has been to split my working days into time I travel to work and days I work from home. On the latter, I usually visit the gym first. I found it was quicker than I imagined it would be to form these new habits, especially as I had been so wedded to my morning routine. I cannot claim any original thought here – I simply based my routine on what I had observed happening to clients over the years and fiddled around in order to combat the issues they had experienced.

Modern technology is the great enabler of remote working, and of course working alone. I would define the former as working away from a central office or business site where you are part of a larger team or organisation, and the latter as working for yourself. Increasingly, courtesy of the power of the internet and modern computer hardware, working for yourself provides the opportunity to collaborate with others who may well be based on the other side of the world. As business becomes more complex and requires access to a wider range of specialist skills, so it is possible to develop an enterprise of substance without employing anyone other than yourself. There are a host of websites for freelance talent such as fiverr and PeoplePerHour and plenty of other alternatives.

The growth of these sites and the capabilities they bring, mean options for finding work and collaborating with others are endless. Furthermore, this way of working also means that the cost of starting a new enterprise has never been cheaper. According to a Lloyds Bank survey form 2016, the average cost of a startup in the UK was £12,000, of which over a quarter was on property or premises, and only a slightly lower amount on transport. In many cases (and I suspect increasingly so) neither of these costs are needed to get you going. It is also important to recognise these are costs for all startups, not necessarily something you might do after reaching normal retirement age.

A good place to start with a new business is to not only to plan well ahead of your normal retirement, but also to start something ahead of your retirement date in a limited or part time capacity. In the USA they like the term "side hustle", personally I am not convinced by the language, but I have yet to find an alternative. This could be as simple as monetising a hobby or passion in a small way to see if it has the capability of providing both an income as well as a purpose to your later years.

When I was looking for a new home, I visited a house on the outskirts of the area where I now live, and was struck by how smartly dressed the gardener was – not only that, he had a brand new lawnmower and was driving an almost new Mercedes estate car. It turns out the gardener had retired and decided to turn his love of gardening into a part time job, both to fulfill his passion, provide variety in what he does and provide a little extra income. Just because you have an executive role and salary does not mean this is what you might do in future. One of the drivers I used a few years ago was a former finance director looking to do something for a couple of days a week.

There are countless opportunities for creating remunerative work beyond normal retirement, too many to note here. Besides, the purpose of this book is to stimulate thought, not provide a "how-to guide". There are plenty of those available already.

We live in a time of almost infinite possibility. Modern technology has developed at such a pace, things that were just a pipe dream a few short years ago are on course to become reality. Things that were once thought impossible are becoming possible. There has never in human history been a better time to be over the age of 60 – imagine then how life will be in 20 years?

What is important to understand about technology is the pace of change. When you are considering your future it is important to acknowledge that you may be able to do something, create something and find purpose in a field that has yet to be developed. So constantly seeking ways to learn and grow will provide your mind with the food it needs to remain healthy.

CONCLUSION

It seems truly extraordinary that, in a period of such rapid change and technological development, society continues to think of retirement in the same way it did 130 years ago. The only allowance for the modern world, structurally at least, seems to be that we are far better off than our ancestors, and many more of us have opportunities that were once the sole preserve of the wealthy.

Although many people have begun to embrace a different type of retirement, our legislators and employers have yet to make the transition – perhaps they never will. Arguably it suits the aims of certain politicians to continue selling a message that at first sounds appealing, but on further examination is both improbable and lacking in benefit to anyone beyond the politicians' own objectives.

Over the last few years, increasing numbers of businesses have closed to new entrants, or even wound up their old style, defined benefit or final salary pension schemes in order to cap, or stop, the ever increasing cost of providing these benefits. The main cause of increasing cost is the life expectancy of scheme members. The alternative pension provision in the form of defined contribution schemes, has largely been less attractive to members, offering a non guaranteed benefit which in many instances may lead to a reduced pension, often in combination with a change to the retirement age.

When faced with the news of changes to pensions in this way, many leap to a mental image of having to live for longer on less. Some naturally recognise a need to work longer – for many this sounds extremely unappealing, especially if they do not enjoy their current employment.

In my life as a financial planner, I have met very many people in their mid-to-late fifties who tell me they want to retire now, or as soon as possible. When I ask why, a staggering number say they do not like what they are doing, or they hate the company they work for. The desire to leave their current role is so strong that focusing their minds on where they might go in life beyond this point can be really hard. Challenging people with questions in an effort to get them to focus on the future (as opposed to fleeing the present), frequently results in them becoming quite annoyed – despite the potential risk to their finances by retiring early. The motivation to run can be overwhelming.

Having left their jobs, it is surprising just how many who of these people quickly become unhappy, or realise they not only need to find work for financial reasons but for their own sanity.

However tempting it might be to want to run away from something, it is important to know where you want to run to. Rather than simply making the knee-jerk decision to leave, there is much to be gained by taking the time to consider where you want to go, and plan ahead. This is essential, both for your finances and your health and welfare.

One of the downsides to increased life expectancy is that increasing numbers of people are spending longer amounts of time in poor health in later life. We owe it to ourselves and our loved ones to live as healthily as we can. By doing so, you enhance your chances of enjoying your later years of freedom and choice.

The demise of the gold-plated pension scheme has, within it, a silver lining. This may seem counter intuitive, however both governments and employers are, in effect, saying to the population at large: "you're on your own". By removing the security of the final salary pension, we are given the chance to plan for ourselves, and the option to direct our own lives – perhaps for the first time ever.

Interestingly, David Blanchett, head of retirement research at Morningstar, states that just three extra years of work can improve your chances of a financially secure retirement by 55%.

Although many people will have made insufficient provision in financial terms for later life, the fact remains that the majority living a more traditional retirement are not suffering from huge money worries. For those that have concerns about money, or are simply in search of a little extra, many have taken it upon themselves to either extend their employment or find part-time (perhaps even multiple) casual roles to meet these needs. The added benefit here is the continued social connection through the workplace. It is very hard to put a price on the value of this.

The overwhelming issue for the recently retired is what to do – how to combat the sense of loss they feel, and how to find their place in society now that the one they had grown comfortable with has been taken away. A study in the USA by Age Wave and

Merrill Lynch found that 62% of those choosing to work beyond retirement age did so in order to stay mentally active.

The fear that precedes retirement is almost always the fear of the unknown, combined with a sense of loss and maybe a sense that our lives are closer to an end. Some of these emotions are entirely understandable. The idea that life is closer to an end might mathematically be true, but as a mindset it is misguided. And in terms of what life is truly about, it could not be further from the truth. One of the great things about getting older is the accumulation of experience and knowledge – choosing positive and impactful ways to use these can lead one to having more life to live, not less.

The change in mindset required to maximise the use of our later lives needs to begin much earlier. We can start by ignoring the convention of retirement. If possible, eradicate the word from your vocabulary. Think instead of living life through a series of transitions. We know that trying to have a very long and fulfilling life as a workaholic is unlikely, so at some point a transition from extreme hours to shorter, more flexible work time is desirable, and will be the norm. Creating a plan of what this looks like for you is therefore one of the best presents you can give yourself.

For some, of course, transition is forced upon them from the outside. Common in the world of work is redundancy. Many employers (and the trades unions representing employees) seem to have developed an odd view of this process when it comes to older workers – or at least that is how their public announcements come across. When organisations make large scale redundancy announcements, they often accompany the announcement with statements declaring a desire to find as many job losses as possible among people prepared to take early retirement. It is as if a little extra in the bank will dispel the anxiety of not knowing what to do tomorrow. It won't.

It is true to say that retirement without money is grim – it is also true to say retirement with only money is dim.

It seems strange that we can identify with the tragic loss of a sporting hero's career cut short by injury, yet we cannot see how this same sense of loss impacts people following a cliff-edge retirement or an enforced early retirement through a redundancy program.

Each individual affected in this way will have a different experience emotionally. A greater awareness in larger businesses of the mental impact is of course helping to address the shock and resulting fallout that redundancy can bring. For the individual, it is important to take action yourself by acknowledging and examining the abilities and skills you possess that can help you with a new future. Remember, these skills may not necessarily be the same as those you have been using in your work – they might only be a small element, or indeed be something you do outside the world of work.

Older workers will find it incredibly hard, if not impossible, to find a new role commensurate with the job lost. There are many reasons of course, but fretting about ageism, or hanging on to a determination to find a job with the same status, income and title is not going to help. It is more likely to prove counter productive. Coping with the loss of status can be hard, however to enable ourselves to move on it is necessary to come to terms with our new reality and adopt a new mindset. After all, the status was conveyed on us by others in the first place.

Although not straightforward, it is possible to create a new place in the world for ourselves. The transition may be tough but if you are prepared to take an open-minded stance on the future, it is possible to move through this phase quickly. One of my favourite words to describe the change in mindset that is needed, is "reframed".

Modern technology, in the form of the microchip, has been the great enabler, a means by which anyone can make a future for themselves, either alone or in collaboration with others. What's more, that collaboration can be with an individual, or group, anywhere on the planet.

I fear our legislators actually want to maintain the status of retirement, as well as the mindset – the one that anyone born from the 1940's onwards was brought up to understand. The reasons might vary, from fear of change to an inability to keep up with the pace of change, as per Boston Consulting Group's remarks about the Bionic Company. Or maybe it is simply that politicians fear loss of control. Whether they like it or not, there is nothing our politicians can do to prevent the march of change, and your ability to make use of it.

Interestingly John Maynard Keynes wrote; "Most people when confronted with a choice of changing their thoughts or proving there is no need to change get busy on the proof." Whilst this clearly applies to those struggling to get fit for later life, or indeed those who have retired, it is also an accurate description of political behavior and never more so than when applied to the concept of retirement.

Keynes also said: "The difficulty lies not so much in developing new ideas as in escaping from old ones."

Although Keynes made these remarks long ago they remain very relevant to the way our lives are being reshaped today. Letting go of that which we have either become comfortable with or have been looking forward to is often the hardest part of letting go. It is hard to make these mental shifts, but in the face of exponential change to the way society and business operates, we must do so. To do so successfully requires us to consider three basic questions for the rest of our lives:

- Where am I now?
- Where am I going?
- How am I going to get there?

Success is a very personal thing and relative to our own experience. Success does not mean you have to become a billionaire or a YouTube sensation – it could be as straightforward as a former executive indulging his love of gardening. Whilst the world might be a competitive place, finding your success in later life is not a competition. What's critical is that whatever you choose to do provides both meaning and purpose to your life.

Given both increased life expectancy and the likelihood of better health for longer, the importance of doing something which has both meaning and purpose for us is crucial to our mental health.

Studies show that retired people waste a great deal of time deciding what they are going to do with the rest of their lives. At 65 a man can expect to live 25 more years and a woman 27. But they can also spend up to 15 years post-retirement reorienting themselves; just 56% say they enjoy retirement "a great deal" during this period and just 57% feel it is working out as they planned.

Wasting the only priceless commodity that exists, time, is to let yourself down significantly. Sadly, mental health issues can impact us all and, like physical health, rob us of time and opportunity. We owe it to everyone in our lives to avoid the unnecessary waste that can accompany lack of planning or thought. Having a future based on luck is not bright.

It would be easy when faced with an unknown future to retreat or withdraw – after all, change is scary. As changes occur with ever-increasing rapidity, life can seem more frightening still. However, just because change looks challenging does not mean it won't happen. Nor will opting out mean you will not get older. As life has an abundance of opportunity, would it not be more sensible and exciting to remain engaged, and enjoy the time you have?

Having made the mindset shift that the model we grew up understanding is broken, it becomes much easier to see a way forward. Letting go can be hard, especially after spending many years contemplating a future that may no longer be an option. However, having made the mindset shift to view the future differently, it is possible to see ways to plan and abundant opportunity. It is only once the clouds are cleared that we can see just how blue the sky really is.

"Blue sky thinking" is a good way to begin considering your future beyond your normal retirement age. This is a time in life when, perhaps even for the first time, you will have complete freedom to exercise choice over what and how you spend your time. Along with the many options of how to spend your time comes the challenge of having to make decisions about those choices. After years of having your schedule dictated to you it is suddenly a requirement to organise yourself. This does not come easily for everyone.

In making choices, it is important for our own wellbeing that those choices lead to an outcome that provides a future with meaning and purpose. We must also ensure that we create a sense of "mattering" in our lives, as referenced earlier in the book. When we matter to others, we create purpose for ourselves, but we also underline our own sense of wellbeing. The size of any future role we might undertake is of no consequence – as long as it matters to us and to others, it will provide purpose and meaning to our lives.

Remaining physically active is central to the longevity of the Okinawans who practice Ikigai. Remaining active does not mean you have to take part in the Grand Canyon rim to rim, or row for miles upon miles everyday, however it does mean getting up and doing something everyday. Everyday tasks, such as walking to the shops, carrying your shopping home, gardening or taking dance classes, are helpful ways to stay active. Remember exercise, like eating and sleeping, needs to be a lifetime habit.

Although I spend much time criticising society for sticking to an old model of life planning, I do like many of the sayings I heard from my grandparents. One simple piece of advice that I am sure you have heard countless times before is, "an apple a day keeps the doctor away". Simple though this is, eating healthily and sensibly is part of the concept of Ikigai. A diet high in fruit and vegetables is part of the culture of those who live in the blue zones and has evolved over time as each generation passes on habits to the next. The Okinawans and Sardinians, aided by the climate and what grows naturally around them, possess something we can all learn from.

According to a recent piece of advice contained in the British Medical Journal of 29th August 2019 vegans need to take supplements to ensure sufficient brain nutrition. The Okinawan diet has been perfected over a very long period of time, and the evidence of the part it plays in their healthy lives and longevity is there for all to see. Sometimes our forebears did know a lot more than we do.

In writing this short book, I have taken into account my many experiences with financial planning clients over what is now a long period of time. Just as they have sought my counsel over the years, so I have sought theirs. I have been fortunate to work with many successful people from all walks of life who have contributed to my understanding of how to help people plan for the future. It is my experience that the happiest among my older clients are those who chose not to retire in the conventional sense but found different ways to reinvent themselves. They are rejuvenated.

Printed in Poland
by Amazon Fulfillment
Poland Sp. z o.o., Wrocław

62500020R00056